CAN DENTISTS BE TRUSTED?

# Martina Evans

*Can Dentists
Be Trusted?*

ANVIL PRESS POETRY

Published in 2004
by Anvil Press Poetry Ltd
Neptune House   70 Royal Hill   London   SE10 8RF
www.anvilpresspoetry.com

This book is published with financial assistance
from Arts Council England

Designed and set in Monotype Bembo by Anvil
Printed and bound in England
by Cromwell Press, Trowbridge, Wiltshire

ISBN 0 85646 376 0

A catalogue record for this book
is available from the British Library

*For Mary Jenkins and David Schiff*

ACKNOWLEDGEMENTS

Some of these poems have previously appeared in
*Agenda, Dreamcatcher, In the Company of Poets* (Hearing
Eye), *Magma,* and in Julia Casterton's *Creative Writing:
A Practical Guide,* 3rd ed. (Palgrave Macmillan) and
*A Step by Step Guide to Writing Poems* (Crowood Press).

I should like to thank the Authors' Foundation for
an award, The Royal Literary Fund for its assistance and
Dr Vangelis and Roulla Tsirba, who saved my tooth.

Last but not least, Jane Young and Tim Fallon for all
their support and the Apple Mac.

# Contents

# Gas

*For Kit*

Little did I think,
nailed by pain
and wandering
squeezing hands
in my first dentist's chair,
that I would be running
down the road
to my second sea-side
dentist
who had great gas
in a cylinder in his surgery.

The third in Munster
to have Relative Analgesia,
Mr Shinkwin didn't believe
in pain. Cold thin air
breathed through a mask
changed the din of the drill
into the pure art
of Jimi Hendrix's guitar
Mr Shinkwin's eyes
blazing blue
as the Atlantic Ocean
that belted against the side
of this small town.

My friend Dolores
rightly worried that
it would come
to the nuns' ears

that my hysterical laughter
had been heard
out on the street.

But instead of my normal
reaction of heart-squeezed
mortification,
I only laughed again,
flashing my silver fillings,
in Hart's shop, Clonakilty,
examining their jewelled jars
and glass cases
buying quarters and quarters
of all different kinds of sweets.

# Jars of Sweets

Shelves and shelves
and ladders to climb,
a broad wooden counter,
a silver scoop for sugar
to be packed
in strong brown paper
bags, loaves wrapped
in newspaper, bread
shaped like the back seat
of a car
and once, like a monkey,
climbing high
to put my hand inside
the jar of Irish Roses.

Red-handed, shame felt
like my stomach was being
taken out, when my mother
called *caught you.*
But there was
no punishment,
instead she told me
how when she was a child
in *her* mother's shop
she took a broom,
swiped the high shelf
and knocked a jar
of acid drops to the ground.

That's where she was
found, down among

the broken glass
and sweets.
It could have been
the broom
and the fact that she was
far bolder than me,
but I couldn't help believing
that my mother was
some kind of a witch.

# Manure

*For Líadáin*

Maybe
it had something
to do with roses,
but somehow
I thought
that the word manure
meant sweet.
Tiptoeing across
the stiletto heel-pocked floor,
I lifted my nose like a dog
to drink in draughts
of my sister's bedroom,
Atrixo, Pond's cold cream,
hairspray and Tweed
parfum de toilette spray.
Now, sea breeze incense,
strawberry lip balm
and toffee lipstick all over
your glitter-spilled pillow
bring back those innocent days
when I would have told you
the same as I told my sister
that your smell
is as nice as
manure.

# A Beige Mini in the Sixties

The smallness of it,
our bare knees poking out
of our corduroy paisley dresses
and the backs of our legs
glued to the warm seats.

The bottle of water for topping up the radiator
that always sat in the side pocket with a bottle of holy water
in the shape of a see-through Virgin Mary.

My brother putting the plastic Virgin to his lips
and drinking down great slugs before driving away
to an exam which he failed anyway.

The crash at the junction of Pine Street
and the fuss that was made of Fifi the dog
by the staff in Casualty
at the North Charitable Infirmary.

Waiting outside the Bank of Ireland while she made her
     lodgement,
dreading the moment we would have to walk up to strangers,
'Excuse me, my mother's just learned to drive,
could you turn our car and face it for home please?'

Shopping by the sea in Clonakilty,
navy 'wet look' patent shoes for my mother,
red shoes with buckles for me.

Fifi hanging her hairy head out the window,
me hanging my boy's haircut out of the window,
the sweet taste of the gulps of flying air.

My mother driving to Limerick
and getting up on the wrong part of the new road,
workmen running after us, shaking their fists.

My father's face
when my mother put her foot on the accelerator
and told him he was at her mercy.

The cloud of gravel
when she drove out of the yard
and the gasps from the men looking out the window.

I can't remember how the Mini died,
only our disgust when she replaced it
with a black Morris Minor for fifty pounds.

She laughed at us and said she didn't care,
*she* wasn't ashamed of it,
she would collect us from the convent in it,
visit us more often in fact.

But in the end the Morris Minor refused to budge,
mocked her view from the kitchen window,
stuck to the stones of the rough ground
where the salesman had parked it.

# On Living in an Area of Manifest Greyness and Misery

*London is a vast ocean in which survival is not certain.*

*Essex Road and the unluckily named Balls Pond Road are areas of manifest greyness and misery.*

from *London: the Biography* by Peter Ackroyd

I sleep high on the bird's nest.
Trucks and lorries shake the house
and make the bricks tremble,
roaring tidal waves rock the bed
and put me to sleep.
There are odd wrecked Georgian houses
beached between tyre shops and takeaways.
Sometimes people are murdered.
Police sirens shriek up and down all day
like seagulls chasing sandwiches.
On the second floor,
we can look right into the 38
and see all the people
but we think they can't see us.
And we can jump on the 38 ourselves,
sail on the top deck
down to Bloomsbury and Victoria.
Our walls are stuffed with horsehair,
on stormy nights we hear the horses gallop.
Like us, they don't want to leave.
The ghost of a cat lives next door.
Young black drivers play hip-hop and dance hall,
when they stop it's a five-minute party
and you never know when it might happen.

The pink-haired squatters dance topless
on the concrete roof when it's hot.
John Ball's pond lies under our back gardens,
the shades of his cows low at full moon.
But it's the roll of traffic
that makes it more of an ocean
especially the sound of rushing wheels
when it rains,
and the uniformed Catholic children
slip along the wet pavement
like blue fish
swimming down the Balls Pond Road.

# The Road to Vesuvius

is twisty,
on the slopes houses are sandwiched
in terraces, painted yellow, salmon
apricot with scarlet or green shutters
pots of fiery geraniums
trailing strands of wisteria
lemon, orange and olive trees,
tomatoes twice as good
as the Turkish ones
according to Nello the guide.
Although the people
have been offered 35,000 Euros
to move, they prefer to stay here
without running water
resting in the hands of God.
Faces exchange glances along the seats
of this grey tourist bus
clinging by its brakes
eight hundred feet above sea level
as if *our* plans will never be interrupted
and we will never be snuffed out
by the thumb of God.

## Sounds of the Sixties

Rain drumming
on the galvanised roof
of the bottle shed,
where my father and I
were slugging from
the heavy brown bottles
of Woodpecker cider
and Cidona
respectively.

The way my father
went *sisssssss*
under his breath
when he didn't like
someone.

My mother snapping
the elastic of her corset
laughing with the relief
of releasing
herself from her clothes
at night-time.

The peremptory bark
of Fifi, demanding
to be lifted
onto the couch.
(On Good Fridays
she managed it herself
when there was nobody
in the house.)

And then the fifth sound,
my breathing bubbling fast
and sweet as
Tanora into a glass,
scudding down the road
from Mass,
back to the Five Find-Outers,
by the range
where I could be
swigging
ginger beer
and sharing out
great big slabs of chocolate
with Fatty and friends.

# No Offence

No offence.
But.
I don't like your mobile
your coat
or your cat.

No offence.
But.
That mattress is lumpy,
the pasta is oily
and I don't like your flat.

No offence.
But.
Your ribs are all ribby,
your stomach sticks out
and when I'm round at your place
I feel a burning need to shout.

And tell the truth.
Because I'm a Christian
and a straight kind of best friend.
No offence if you don't like it,
it's my nature to offend.

# The Day My Cat Spoke to Me

*For Geraldine More O'Ferrell*

I was surprised not so much by the fact
that she spoke
but by the high opinion she had of me.
'I think you're great,' she said
and it was at this point
I looked at her in surprise.
'I mean,' she continued, 'the way
you've managed to write anything at all!
Fifteen court hearings
and that barrister,
the way she looked at you.'
'But you weren't there,' I said.
'Oh but I can imagine it,' said Eileen,
her yellow eyes opening wide
before narrowing into benevolent slits.
'I only had to look at you,
gulping down your red lentil soup
when you came home after nearly three
hours in the witness box defending
your right to write.
I could see it all in every swallow you took,
her butty legs and her manly shoulders
in that black suit, did she have dandruff?
I hope not, because it really shows up on black.
Saying those things to you,
*Oh Miss Cotter we would all like the luxury
of sitting at home writing books!*
Holding up paper evidence between finger
and thumb, *Here is another job
you failed to get Miss Cotter.*

Trying to make you go out to work
with radiation in a hospital
and who would take care of us?
What would the cats of this house
do without the sound of your pen scratching
on paper, the hum of your computer,
your lovely lap and the sound of you
on the telephone?
The big dyed blonde head of her!
And where did she think she was going?
Well, earning a lot of money for her own words
by the looks of things.
And saying them to you!
The best writer that ever heaved a can of Tuna
or opened a pack of Science Plan.
And as Mary Jenkins said about him
who paid for the terrible utterances
"It's just as well that Shakespeare wasn't married to *him*."
And then when he was in the witness box, he wished
you the best of luck with your writing . . . '
At this point Eileen paused, closed her eyes.
I was waiting for her to say something witty herself.
After all it was a great opportunity for irony
which for some reason I have always
associated with cats.
But when she opened her eyes again
she requested a scoop of softened butter
after which she licked her lips in detail
and hasn't opened her mouth since
if you don't count yawning, lapping,
eating, washing, miaowing
and screeching at intruders.

## Oldest Friend

He brought me books.
So tall, he had to have
his shoes specially made for him.
His eyes were brown.

And his hair was silver.
I walked beside him
I talked to him,
I was a tomboy in shorts.
He had daughters.
I wanted to be his son.

I copied the way he spoke
*Christ it's cold* and
*would ya*
*look at that hoor.*
He swore when nobody did
and he made it
swashbuckling.

His dogs were Lucky
and Cindy, their pink
tongues lap water
from Double Diamond ashtrays
as if it was yesterday.
But it was 1969.

Cindy was Lucky's mother.
Lucky looked like the white terrier
in the ad
for Black and White Scotch.

Boxes of books
and tea and cakes from Thomson's,
a suit of armour,
a revolver on the wall,
he lived in the oldest house
in Mallow.

When the cancer
caught his throat,
I saw his wife on the street.
She was making him sherry trifle.
She was going to whip it hard
she said.

When he died, I didn't talk about it.
I heard them saying that I didn't care.
The oldest house in Mallow
is a block of flats now.
I never want to see it.

# The Rabach

It was the father,
the old Rabach
who put him
up to it.

So the Rabach
killed the sailor
who'd come so deep
into the glen,
two hour's walk
from the road.

Under the shadow
of Tooth Mountain,
the sailor came for shelter,
up rocks
as big as carts,
plunging through the bog,
striped slugs and rushes
until the sheer walls
of stone closed him in.

The Rabach hid the body,
under the hearth stone,
leaned out
in the early morning,
to smoke a good pipe.

---

NOTE   Rabach is the Irish for violent or vigorous, both of which
are appropriate in this case. The Rabach lived on the Beara
Peninsula in the early part of the nineteenth century.

Gatekeepers and painted ladies
skimmed the bog,
grasshoppers gritted
among the purple loosestrife,
spotted orchids
and feverfew.

It was only a scut
of an English deserter
who wouldn't have the gumption
to haunt him.

There could be peace here now
with the pipits and the wagtails,
the sound of that hum
across the bog.

Except why did Mary Sullivan
have to be doing
the good woman
getting up at five
to draw fresh water
for tea?

Tea for her long-nosed
so-and-so of a husband
for his two-day journey,
on a horse too good for him,
to the Butter Exchange
in Cork.

The houses were too close
in this stone room of a glen.

She'd seen him
at that hour
through the deep small
square window, blessed
herself and said
nothing.

Until the day
she had a row
with the Rabach
and he pushed her
into the heather
and meadowsweet.

She'd had her warning
that afternoon.
Along the side
of the mountain
stones cast a shadow face
real and hard,
with an overhanging brow.

Yet she couldn't keep it
to herself,
the wet scramble up
from the ground.
His hard blue stare.

*I could put you away for good.*

He followed her,
choked her with a spancel
and she stared
at the holly tree that grew

out of the cleft
of a rock.

There were no other trees
only rocks and stones.

Upside down in the stream
to make it look like drowning,
she was in no position
to put anyone away for good.

Afterwards he went down
to Glanmore Lake,
rinsed the sweat
off his face and hands.
Smoked another fine pipe.

The bright long-bodied
damsel flies
over the rocks,
if he was a scholar
he'd know the word
in Irish to describe
the exact stamp
of that bursting blue.
There was great heat
there that day,
great comfort in the rays
drying his face.

Some foreign blackguards
had shot the swan's mate.
The Rabach sat on a flat rock
and cried for the one swan

going round and round
the lake.

Little knowing
that some big *búdán*
of a copper miner
from Allihies
had been up the hill
and saw him at Mary.

The miner only kept quiet
because he'd been stealing
cow's tails himself,
it was on his death bed
that he started his pillallooing.
Told the priest.

That was when
the Tally Ho started.
A whole year
he was on the run
and it was no joke
up high in a cave,
cold, afraid to light
a fire, sending triple
echoes across the rocks
to scare them off.

Mists came right up
to the mouth
of *Pluais an Rabach**

---

* cave of the Rabach

white veils hanging
like sheets on a line
in front of him.
If he was a couple
of inches taller, he thought
he'd be able to see right
over the top of them.

The heather changing,
the harebells,
wild bitter apples,
snow, then snowdrops,
bog cotton and the bluebell,
the Virgin Mary's own flower.

Everywhere there were scattered
split and scored rocks and boulders
behind which a hundred men
could hide.

Mary Sullivan's son
was growing up too,
he gave the tip,
knowing the special day
when the Rabach
would be at home
with his wife.

Her labour was hard,
he had to break
a three-legged stool
to keep out the sound
of her pain.

Across the bog,
the soft brown hares
were hopping. They said
that the hares had big giant
cousins in Van Dieman's Land.

You'd see them if you got transported.

Her pain caught him in the throat,
he couldn't even smell the wild flowers
or hide from the blaze of redcoats
that blew up around the house.

He wouldn't look at them
when they tied him.

He kept his two blue eyes fixed
on the holly tree
and on the cracked and scattered
boulders behind which a hundred men
could hide.

They said that he was the last man
to be hanged in Munster.
They said when they opened
him up afterwards,
he had two hearts.

# Ink

Our copybook covers
were decorated with round towers,
swallows and old Irish letters,
I hoped every new one
would be the one
I would keep clean.

As clean as the milk-white inkwells
that fitted into the holes
on top of our old-fashioned desks
like upside-down top hats.

The dark blue ink
swayed and swelled
inside the china-white bowls
but never spilled
no matter how much commotion
there was.

And there was
a lot of commotion,
with boys being chased
round the desks by the Master,
getting kicked in the stomach
and locked into cupboards.

I was slapped so much
my fingers felt like
great foreign sausages bursting out
of their flimsy ink-stained skins.

Being so bold
it was a surprise
to get the honour of filling the wells
from the great earthenware pot
that was the colour of Goldgrain biscuits.

But the pleasure of holding its sandy lip
to each gleaming white brim
was never realised.
I dropped the pot
before I got to the first one.

*That inkpot's been in this school*
*for over a hundred years, Miss Cotter*
*and it would take you to break it!*

The Master was so astounded
he forgot to beat me,
just left me standing there
with the stain spreading round
my feet,
the fall of ink so heavy
the mark was still there
when I checked twenty years later.

# Mothers' Monologue

Yes, you have to be very careful what you transfer onto your child.

That's a nervous cough, that is.

It really could be you that is causing that cough, you know. The child is a barometer of the mother.

Well, when she comes round here, she eats everything on her plate.

Yes, I just visualise his first wife and I find the peace.

Ever since I became a Christian.

I know, yes, really, apparently she was being horrible to my Polly.

Have you done the homework?

You absolutely can't be serious! Those potatoes we never touch them in South America, English potatoes we call them. No, she needs sweet potato.

Well, the thing with children is that if they know they have no choice you'd be surprised what they eat.

She is just attention seeking, you have to be careful, she is taking control. Yes there is a really interesting book about that syndrome. Remind me to lend it to you.

It is very wrong to make her do the violin. These things can't be forced.

You have to take control, cover the lit tray, then Eileen will have to go in the garden. So what if she doesn't like muddy paws! Show her who's boss.

I just visualise him in pink and then everything is alright.

You have to rise above it.

Mmmm, I can't believe your bad luck, you must have very bad karma.

Yes, if you look in the Old Testament you will see there is an absolute certainty about Vegans.

If you know your blood group then you can figure out what phase of evolution you are from. For instance group O hunter-gatherer you need to keep away from grains.

Well, if you really like bread, that is actually a sign that you shouldn't be eating it.

Visualise yourself in a long blue cloak with red lining . . . you are approaching a stream, you've got your bundle of worries.

Place it carefully beyond the curtain of water.

I sodding well visualised his ex-wife and now her photographs are all over the kitchen table.

Well *they* are at fault. This school and the people at this school give me the pip.

They are a total bunch of loopy hippies and they can't manage a piss-up excuse my French in a brewery.

Soooooo flaky.

Well, it is true I couldn't get her in anywhere else.

No, I just pray for peace, I pass the problem on to God.

Oh, I've changed since I have been a Christian.

Mmmmmm, yes, yes, *yes*. It's all about letting go.

But I have a right to my feelings.

The hell I will forgive. That horrible woman, who does she think she is? I'm going to have a word with her tonight, I am.

What's wrong? Oh you have noticed. Does my worry show that much?

I have reason to be worried. The moon is in Scorpio.

# Seven Glimpses of a Tall Dead Friend

An avenue of lime trees
wreathing over our heads.

Tan sandals strapped
over white ankle socks.

Two silver crosses glittering
on identical beds of royal blue velvet.

Two white Holy Communion dresses
one long, one short.

One tall girl with her back to the wall,
streaks of blood
on the mushroom-coloured wainscot.

One short girl rushing forward
like a bull to butt the Master.

Thrown out for no good reason
the tall one behind the hedge
of the church of St John the Baptist,
kneeling on wet grass,
shivering, and red-haired
like the virgin
in Dante Gabriel Rossetti's
*Annunciation*,
already a ghost.

# Trail

The high notes
of petrol
when the BP man
came to steep the dipstick
in the tanks.

The rubber leather
gauntlets
kept for that purpose
in the corner
of the windowsill
of the shop.

The burnt shiny
black crusts
of the grinder loaves
as they were brought in
on trays
by Teddy the Breadman.

The whiff of gloss
from the painter
John Brown who
ruined the dining room table
while we were busy
listening to his
lightning conversation.

Brown and black Nugget shoe polish
on dull moist shoes
lining up for their shine

Saturday evening
before being taken
by our legs to Mass
on Sunday morning.

Half a bottle
of turpentine
to be inhaled deeply
on the spot
where it stood,
the shoe shelf
in the bottle shed.

The tang
from Eileen Dennehy's
tin of Mr Sheen,
the way she did
housework
like a girl
on springs.

Hay and cats
in the cat shed
Guinness and Power's
whiskey after Mass.
Toast.
And the way
hot ironed sheets
were like
toast.
Burying my face
in new books
the sweetish
yellowness

of the soft pages
of old books
in the mobile library,
all of them
beckoning.

# There is a Room

*When I die I will return to seek*
*The moments I did not live by the sea*

SOPHIE DE MELLO BREYNER

It has always been waiting for me,
long windows down to the dusty floorboards,
golden brown tea as good as I drank
out of pink and white cups
in the Convent of Mercy thirty years ago.
John McCormack playing on the record player,
hot cross buns and butter,
the ocean below rising in silver grey sheets
same colour as my coat
which hangs by the door.
In a moment, I'll put it on,
walk along the sand
and the spray will be like silk on my face.

# Catholic Mothers' Monologue

Well, it's the best education there is, it's the discipline.

If I had a million pounds I wouldn't pick any other school.

Well, maybe if I had the money, maybe that school in Hampstead.

Oh Father, when we sang *Be Thou My Vision!*

Don't let her think there's a choice about it. Jesus, if you start off with her thinking that she can get away with not going to Mass, God alone knows where she'll end up!

I just get Jack into that pew, come hell or high water. I give him a big tube of Pringles, it keeps him quiet and by the time he's worked his way down through them, Mass is nearly over.

You see, you have peace of mind, you know they're getting the best education.

Well as Eamon said to me the other night, no one talks about the good Christian Brothers.

Of course there is, there's nothing like seeing your daughter coming down the aisle in her First Holy Communion dress, isn't that right, Father?

Father Flynn with his fecking sandwiches, they think we've nothing else to do. Just because we want to get into the school.

Margaret is down in the centre every Sunday, roasting chickens for winos, just because she wants to get the son in before he gets stabbed at the Comprehensive.

And they're determined to make an accountant of him anyway and why wouldn't they?

So, well, we were determined to find out if she was bringing her to Mass in London and when we brought her up to the cloakroom, Patsy asked and the child didn't know what Mass was.

If she was bringing the child to Mass, they wouldn't have half the problems they have.

So they are driving round in their Volvos with boots full of drink. That was bought by the funds, drinking the funds. In their big Volvos!

It would make you mad.

And it's their children who get to be serving on the altar.

It's no trouble, Father, so like ten rounds of ham and ten rounds of egg, will that be enough?

Well, Kathleen is a teacher, she knows what is suitable for a child and it's not all this spoiling. She told me herself what she would do.

Isn't it desperate? As if it was bad enough with the pair of them split up, but those grandparents will never see her coming down the aisle in a white communion dress.

In any kind of white dress, probably. And never see an altar again, either.

It's the grandparents who suffer the most and I'd know being a grandmother.

Ah, it's very sad, but as I said, if there's alcohol involved. There isn't a chance. Pity, she waited until she was nearly forty.

So they stole the funds and now Father Tim is all over the tabloids and to think I was down there clearing his garden for him, yes Father and No Father and himself and the secretary at it the whole time.

I nearly had a hernia getting into that school.

What's she going to do now she's taken the child out?

But it's a shame, it's a shame, half of it is they can't be
bothered to put themselves out. Too lazy to go to
Mass.

I had to pay Aisling two pounds a week to get her to go
to the Communion classes and I couldn't even tell
you how much the dress cost.

But now we have the video and no one can take that
away from us.

I burst into tears when I heard the organ starting up *Be
Thou My Vision* and didn't I start off again at the
reception? I couldn't help it when Father Flynn
thanked me again for the sandwiches in front of
everybody.

# For I will Consider My Cat Eileen Murphy

*After Christopher Smart*

For I am annoyed with her.

For she doesn't kiss My Cat Alice in kindness.

For she bullies Alice and pushes her off high walls.

For she is only interested in her own coat.

For she sucks up to visitors and ignores me.

For she strikes the centre of my back to wake me if she
thinks there is a hope of tuna.

For Alice cringes when she approaches.

For she roars for her food and reprimands me.

For her hairs cause too much work with the hoover and
the roll of sellotape.

For she will always desert me for patches of sunlight.

For she runs away from me in front of the neighbours.

For she clings to my lap when she is only looking for a
heat-up.

For her colours – soft grey, fawn, shining white, honey,
sand, gold, black and peach – laugh in the face of
designers and manufacturers.

For she sought out Líadáin when Líadáin was very sad and pressed herself against Líadáin's side in á such way that tenderness could not be mistaken.

For she has the outline of a tiara marked out on the top of her head.

For the length and strength of her whiskers are the proof of God's bounty.

For we know that she doesn't pretend.

For she is a striped stravaganza with a tiara on her head.

For she gives a damn.

## Walking on Snow

Defender of the cat flap,
who thundered
at intruders
formed your paws
into fists
and beat the perspex
flap back and forth,
where are you now?

Your shell lies
in the earth
cold, stiff
and narrow
in a small box
while I sit here,
looking out,
instinctively waiting
for your spring
to the back of my seat.

I had foreseen
all the other disasters
except this,
your wasted body
in my hands
your last cry of protest
when the vet slipped
the needle
in the IV line.

Even when I knew
it was malignant

I still did not know
the meaning of malignancy;
a growth whose advance
one could see
from the morning
to the afternoon.

Death came
like a salesman
with his foot in the door.
And you didn't want to go.
And I wasn't ready.
Like the young fox
who wasn't ready for snow.

Two weeks
after your death,
snow falling
all over our garden
and next door,
over your grave,
the patio, the lawns,
the gravel.

A small scared fawn
and white fox
turning and twisting
from patio
to lawn and gravel
leaving criss-cross tracks
turning and twisting
in his vain attempt
to avoid
walking on snow.

# Some Bores are Just Born

Why are you wearing those trousers?

My mother is famous in America.

I'm going to get three new pairs of jeans and a jumper and four tops at the weekend. My granddad gave me three hundred pounds.

And he bought me a huge encyclopaedia. All the boys hate your new clothes, I went round and asked them all and they all said it and I said she's my best friend. All the boys like me best, they said it at break time. You look so weird in that coat and your small head in that hat. Lyra said so.

Please, I'm speaking and anyway there I was and I broke my leg and I couldn't walk and the teachers were horrible to me.

That book looks really boring and that German teacher, she's horrible, she doesn't know her job. I don't mind telling her either.

But I couldn't believe how horrible he was to you.

Why is your mother slapping those playing cards so hard on the table?

Why is she always playing Patience when I come around?

Oh, yes, well I've been to France seventeen times.

She is horrible, she is.

And rude, too. You are mental, but please you are, please I'm speaking, it's very rude to interrupt, my very best friend.

# Golfer

If bulls' eyes were blue
you could have sold
the Golfer's eyes by the quarter
cold, sweet and glassy
like something you would suck.

For comfort.

He always said the same things
perched on the red covered seat
under the black and white television,
claws holding tight
to a tin of Condor tobacco.
*That was Beethoven's fifth*
*in D Minor*
*Marilyn was always the nicest one*
*of the Monroes.*

Growing up in a bar
or even habitually drinking there,
you could get pure sick of that kind of thing.

Boarding school meant I had friends
my own age, with me all day long,
novels hidden in cunning brown paper covers,
no one taking them off me, telling me to
*Go down to the bar and talk to the customers.*

Not to mention the amount of sweet eating
I could get away with – a pineapple chunk
stuck in the corner of each cheek,

nights given over to the flavours of raspberry
blackberry and the mysterious (in the dark at any rate)
delights of Quality Street.

I wouldn't have said I was lonely
walking in line to Confession
talking incessantly to Joan and Dolores
about *The Hungry Hill, Gone with the Wind*
and the relative merits of Yorkshire Toffee
and Emerald sweets.

But they were surprised when a tramp passed
and I broke from the ranks, shouting
*Golfer! Golfer!*
shouting again and again
until he turned round to see
a school girl
forty five miles from home,
waving and shouting at him
in the middle of the street.

# Taste

Tomato sandwiches
two or three hours
old
eaten on the grass
by a brown river
washed down
with a bottle of
Clock House
red lemonade.

Fat bursty
chipolatas grilled
under the gas
Saturday mornings
fresh from
the Denny's Meat Man's
delivery.

Campbell's sweet
Cream of Tomato soup
spooned onto
my rapturous tongue
that thanked God
I was a Catholic
so that I could have
this meat-stock-free treat
for lunch every Friday.

Campbell's Cream of Celery soup
that gave rise
to my mother's

fear that I might
be a nine-year-old
alcoholic
when I asked
for another spoon
of sherry in my bowl.

# Three Reasons for Getting Disgusted with Popular Songs

The plumber
whose favourite song
was Aretha Franklin's *Respect*
and who walked over everyone
in the house
including young children.

The husband
who refused to let his wife go,
curling himself into a drunken
ball, declaring that *like*
*a bird on a wire he had tried*
*in his way to be free.*

And the man
who loved his country,
singing of murders
committed by braver men
in order that he could
dangle off a bar stool
warbling *The Foggy Dew.*

# Paddy from Dingle

No one knew
what drove him out
on the road
but no one
messed with him
when he strode in
and stood
with peeled blue eyes
at the counter.

And no one
stood anywhere near him
when he threw darts
from twice the normal distance,
his shabby-suited back
to the gilt-framed mirror
on whose shining lake
glided the faces of people
wincing.

Darts shot through the air,
headlong like arrows
reflected sideways
in the other mirror
that lay behind
the optic measures,
the upside down
bottles of Scotch
and Power's and Paddy,
pewter tankards, statues
of hurlers and Scottie dogs,

stacks of the green and white
and red and white
Major and Carroll's cigarettes,
red and black
safety matches
and playing cards
that lay waiting
to be brought to life
between the fingers
of the evening crowd.

By evening, Paddy
would be on the road again,
having clapped his cap
on his head,
cutting strides
into darkness and wind,
his lips moving repeatedly,
up to his hilt
in communications
with another world.

No one noticed
for a while
that he was gone
completely
and not mentioned again
much until
John Paul the Second
was elected
and someone remarked
that the new pope
was the head off
Paddy from Dingle.

# Burning Rubbish

A peachy sunset
over a line of black fir trees,
fires all over our field.
I am there in shorts and sandals
running with a can of petrol
to revive the drooping flames,
my father's solid body
standing still among the blazes
like a Roman general,
just here, this evening
for once
like a king.

# Forty Five

My head eventually grew
over the top
of the biscuit and white
formica table in the bar
and I could see them there
playing forty five.

Big red hands with cuts
and grazes and crumpled
fingers, clutching cards
that had to be slammed
to the table with thumps
and cracks of bone
and hahs of triumph.

I, too,
wanted to have a blazing face
when I threw down the
gauntlet of a Joker or a five
and in the winter dark evenings
Tom Twomey, Bill Drummy
and Paddy the Priest played
Beggar my Neighbour, Old Maid
and even forty five with me.

I was ignorant
of the crucial fact
that gabbing
was worse than reneging,
but they listened, even laughed
and played politely,

keeping their energies
for the evening feast.

Then I hid out
on the window sill
wrapping
the red velvet curtains
round me
like an Angel
that would appear
in a biblical land,
peering out at a world
of passion and precision
I could not understand.

Set jaws, spellbound fists, gleeful flings,
blue eye after blue eye
after brown eye,
all holding their whist.
Angel Gabriel could have come
and blown his trumpet off,
the Second Coming
could have come and gone,
they wouldn't have heard a thing.

# Song of Sweets

Rolls of Red Toffo
stuck to the roof
of my mouth like
communion and
the pink thin strips
of Long John Silver
chewing gum
could be kept between
the pages of a book.

Pineapple bars were broken
in half by smashing them
against the school stone
wall and the halves stuck
out of my cheek
like slabs of concrete.

Urney bars were
the sweetest
a different coloured
piece of fondant
in every chocolate square
and I never knew
which colour was coming.

Sour grapes chewing gum
could make my eyes stream
with the joy of sourness
my brace abandoned
in order to give myself
up to them, completely.

Broken scrumble sold
by the quarter,
milk chocolate-covered peanuts
pear drops Catch bars and Yorkies
were for later forays out of
boarding school.

But now, at age eight,
to live in a shop
for the duration of Lent
was crucifixion
just for me
who could be found on Easter Nights
feet trembling on the cold red tiles
of the bathroom
throwing the whole lot up.

# Can Dentists Be Trusted?

*For Tatiana and Peter*

There are the ones
you only visit once,
like the fellow
in Phibsboro, Dublin
who roared *Jesus Fucking Christ*
his leg up on the dentist's chair
as he pulled out
my embarrassed tooth.

Or the one who told me to lie
about being pregnant
so I could have crowns
that I never said
I wanted
free on the NHS.

The man in Kensington
who told me he loved
the Irish, really
then died five years later
leaving me the legacy
of an HIV test.

Others, you have to stay with.
But if they are private
they may want all your teeth
in the end.
You could find yourself
opening wide

while laid out on the chair
like a corpse
with a coin in its mouth
travelling
towards the underworld.

## Also by Martina Evans from Anvil

࿊

## *All Alcoholics Are Charmers*

Evans's great skill is in knowing how much to put into a poem. She has a talent for selecting only the most resonant memories, for not over-icing the cake of sentiment. . . .

*All Alcoholics Are Charmers* turns out to be rich in splendidly concise evocations of what it feels like to be Irish in England, in all its quiddity, including the encounters with new cultures on your doorstep . . . Above all, Evans puts the right words in the right order, a dictum whose simple phrasing embodies its demands.

Michael Duggan in *PN Review*

She evokes the pains, fantasies and preoccupations of an Irish Catholic childhood and youth, with an Irish tongue for a story and Irish humour, but uses the theme to show what it's like to be alive. . . . The poems are little dramas and monologues that go straight to the grudges, disappointments, root-confusions and hangups, showing the depths in trivial things and the trivial in the deep. She writes clean narratives, with nothing but factual adjectives, and all the details part of someone's experience, making the book a pleasure to read and recommend.

Herbert Lomas in *Ambit*